THE ILLUSTRATED
Dog's Life

THE ILLUSTRATED

Dog's Life

Warren Eckstein
with
Andrea Simon

FAWCETT COLUMBINE · NEW YORK

A Fawcett Columbine Book
Published by Ballantine Books

Published in the United States by Ballantine Books, a
division of Random House, Inc., New York, and distributed
in Canada by Random House of Canada Limited, Toronto.
Originally published in Great Britain by
Guinness Publishing Ltd. in 1992.

Library of Congress Catalog Card Number: 92-52664

ISBN: 0-449-90669-8

Manufactured in the United States of America
First American Edition: November 1992

10 9 8 7 6 5 4 3 2 1

CONTENTS

INTRODUCTION

While we are not certain when humans and dogs first came together, we do know this alliance is thousands of years old. As the oldest domesticated animals, dogs have been both deified and damned through various periods of history. Ultimately, dogs earned and have maintained their title as "man's best friend."

THE DOG AS A DEITY

Evidence of dog worship has been found in many parts of the world — the Ancient Egyptians, for example, regarded the dog as a symbol of fidelity and as a guardian god. In Lower Egypt, where the lives and prosperity of the people depended on the annual flooding of the Nile River, the bright "dog-star" Sirius never failed to herald the flood's approach. Egyptians relied on its appearance as a warning that it was time to move their herds and themselves to higher ground in anticipation of the flooding of the river.

Anubis, the Egyptian god with the head of a dog or a jackal, was one of the most important gods of the underworld. His duty was to attend to the ritual preparation of the bodies of the dead, to weigh the heart of every man or woman on the scale of justice, and to judge people's good and bad deeds on earth before they passed onto the hereafter. In the ancient city of Cynopolis (which actually means "dog city" in Greek), dogs were often sacrificed at special religious festivals dedicated to Anubis. Archeological expeditions reveal that mummified dogs were buried with great ceremony in specially built tombs designed to honor them before this great canine god.

The inhabitants of Ancient Mexico also believed that dogs were entrusted with the task of guiding the dead to the hereafter. Consequently a dog was killed upon the death of his owner, and the body placed beside the owner's to guarantee that the dead person would be guided safely to the other world. Conversely, instead of escorting the spirits of the dead, Cerberus (the three-headed dog of Greek mythology) guarded the gates of Hell to prevent the spirits of the dead from escaping.

THE OBJECT OF SCORN

While dogs took their place among the gods in many religions and cultures, they were considered "unclean" in the Old Testament and in early Christianity — in fact, virtually every reference to them is of a negative nature. For instance, the Old Testament suggests that the most horrible fate that could befall a person at death was not be buried, but to be eaten as offal by the dogs of the street. They did not fair much better in the New Testament, either: Matthew VII, 6 says, "Give not that which is holy unto the dogs, neither cast ye your pearls before swine." It is no wonder that the word "dog" or "cur" became a derogatory term!

During the Middle Ages, the myths of devil-dogs and werewolves developed — the black dog, in particular, appears in many legends of European witchcraft. In fact, the dog-demon was considered to be of higher status than the cat-demon.

In some areas it is still believed that the howling of a dog is a herald of death. There are many versions of this superstition; one version has it that the dogs howl when the Angel of Death passes by, another that two howls mean a man's death, and three howls mean a woman's death while yet others that dogs howl when they see coffins in the air, and that a corpse will be brought from the direction toward which a dog howls.

THE EMBODIMENT OF LOYALTY

Throughout history dogs have been the symbols of loyalty. One of the most famous stories of canine loyalty is recounted in Homer's epic poem *The Odyssey*. Ulysses' dog Argus spent the happy days of his youth hunting with his master but was left behind when Ulysses set forth on his journey to Troy. Many years later when Ulysses returned from his travels disguised as a beggar no one recognized him, except for Argus. Crippled with age and suffering from neglect, Argus recognized his master's voice and crawled to him. After licking the hand of his master, Argus died. Homer wrote of Ulysses' devastation at the loss of the only friend who had not forgotten him.

Although Moslems consider the dog "unclean," they do tell of the legend of Kitmer. Kitmer guarded the seven noble youths of Ephesus while they were asleep; he watched over them for 309 years without pausing for food or water. This dog was rewarded for his service with a place in Paradise.

A more recent story of canine loyalty is the story of Greyfriars Bobby. This little Skye terrier accompanied his Scottish master to Edinburgh every market day. After his master died in 1858 and was buried in Greyfriars churchyard, Bobby would lie by his master's grave. He spent nearly ten years at the graveside, until he died at the age of fourteen. His years of faithfulness are memorialized in a statue erected in Greyfriars churchyard which is simply inscribed, "A tribute to the affectionate fidelity of Greyfriars Bobby."

ORIGINS OF BREEDS

Debate will never cease as to the true ancestry of modern-day dogs. Some experts argue that all of them share the wolf as their common ancestor; others theorize that, while some breeds of dogs originated from wolves, others can be traced back to jackal-type antecedents.

Today, The American Kennel Club, the chief registering body of purebred dogs in the United States, recognizes 134 breeds and varieties of purebreds. These breeds are divided into six groups: sporting dogs (including various types of Spaniels, Retrievers, Setters and Pointers), hounds (including Beagles, Dachshunds and Whippets), working dogs (including Old English Sheep Dogs, Boxers and Rottweilers), terriers (including Miniature Schnauzers, and Airedales and Cairn Terriers), toy dogs (including Yorkshire Terriers, Pugs and Pomeranians), and non-sporting dogs (including Chow Chows, Dalmatians and Poodles). Many countries, among them Canada and the United Kingdom, have their own kennel clubs and breed classifications. Because breeds may be popular in one era and then decline in popularity in another, these clubs will occasionally recognize new breeds, and drop or reclassify others.

COATS OF MANY COLORS

Labrador Retrievers originally accompanied every Newfoundland fishing boat and were trained to jump overboard as the boats neared land, gather the fish-filled nets in their mouths, and swim ashore. Regardless of whether their outercoats are black, yellow or chocolate, all Labrador Retrievers sport wooly, water-resistant undercoats that protect them from the elements.

drop or reclassify others.

In addition to the purebreds recognized by various kennel clubs, many other breeds exist. Their exclusion on the clubs' rosters is usually due to lack of popularity or the relative scarcity of the breed. And, last but not least, we must never forget dogs of mixed parentage. Referred to as "mongrels," "mutts," "mixed breeds" they provide us with just as much companionship, love and assistance as their purebred relatives.

CANINE VARIATIONS

In no other species of animal do so many physical variations and mutations exist. If you were to observe a series of domestic cats, you would quickly conclude that, aside from their coats, their silhouettes were basically the same. One cannot say this about our dogs. For instance, compare the short-legged, sausage-shaped Dachshund to the long-legged streamlined form of the majestic Borzoi. It is hard to fathom that both breeds are members of the same species, yet they are! The same can be said when comparing the long-nosed, silky coated Afghan Hound to the short-haired, flat-faced Pug, or the tiny, Mexican Hairless dog to

the massive, wavy-coated Bernese Mountain dog.

Even among the same breed of dog you will find different coat colors and different textures. Dachshunds, for example, come in three coat textures — Smooth, Wirehaired and Longhaired. The same goes for the Collie, which comes in Rough-coated and Smooth-coated varieties. Even when the coat texture remains consistent, the coloration may vary greatly within the same breed. A perfect example of this is the Great Dane whose coat may be fawn, blue, black, brindle (brown with black stripes) or harlequin (white with black spots).

Indeed, centuries of man's selective breeding practices have certainly left their mark. But regardless of his particular appearance, every dog remains "man's best friend."

UNCONDITIONAL LOVE

One of the wonderful things about our dogs is their total acceptance of us and our world, even when we seem large and menacing to them. No matter how bad a day we've had, or how badly we think we look, they still have a special greeting for us. All they ask from us in return is love, care, and companionship.

HIDDEN DANGER

These little fellows have been allowed exposure in their owner's garden. But even such adventures are full of potential hazard — the list of plants harmful to puppies is very long. Many experts recommend that puppies be kept indoors until a week after they have received their first vaccinations against the most common canine ailments. Check with your local nursery or garden center regarding the toxicity of plants.

THE PUPPY

TO BREED OR NOT TO BREED

While the cuteness of puppies may tempt owners to breed their dogs, it is best to spay or neuter them. The reasons are two-fold. First, the canine over-population problem is rampant. A visit to any shelter or humane society will reveal how severe a problem it is. In addition to older dogs, there will be plenty of puppies just waiting for loving homes. Second, studies have shown that spaying the female and neutering the male may decrease the risks of certain health problems later in life.

The only exception is the pedigree bitch that you've decided to breed. In this case, you will be able to witness for yourself the miracle of canine pregnancy and birth.

IN THE BEGINNING

Your bitch will be pregnant for about 63 days, give or take a week. When she is having her litter she may want you around, or she may decide she wants her privacy — respect her wishes. During pregnancy, you should increase her feedings by about a third to a half, in more frequent and smaller quantities, and give her more protein to promote lactation. Finally, make sure she continues to take exercise, and at her own pace. She will probably be able to manage the birth process herself; however, you may want to observe from a distance in case your assistance is needed. Be prepared for a wait. Fifteen to thirty minutes is the average delay between the birth of each puppy, although up to two hours is considered normal.

Each puppy will arrive in its own membranous sac. The mother will pull this off, and immediately clean the puppy's nose and mouth, thus enabling him to draw his first breath. She will then chew off the umbilical cord, severing this pre-natal connection. Within minutes following the last puppy's delivery, Mother will expel the afterbirth. It is not unusual for her to eat the placenta as it contains many nutrients. Finally, she will give the newborn a thorough wash — the licking action of her tongue will serve to stimulate the puppy's circulation and respiration — and then she will settle down to wait for the next arrival.

Shortly after birth, the puppy will find his way to his mother's nipples, and will affix himself to one for his first meal. Mother's milk, called colostrum, contains the protective antibodies needed by the puppy during his first weeks of life.

RAPID DEVELOPMENT

Compared to the development of human babies, puppies grow at an incredibly rapid rate. This is evidenced by the fact that they are so fragile and helpless at birth and they will do little other than sleep and suckle for the first week of their lives.

By the time the puppies are two or three weeks old, their aural and visual senses now functioning, they will be able to move about. At first they are delightfully unsteady on their tiny legs — watching them take their first wobbly steps is truly comical. But by three weeks they will be walking more purposefully, having become accustomed to using their legs, and having increased their strength by almost constant meals at Mother's nipple.

By a month or so after birth, the puppies will have made an incredible transformation from helpless infants to running roly-poly terrors. Mom will no longer enjoy peace. Instead, she'll keep a watchful eye on their antics, and will scold them if she thinks they are being over-confident. It is up to you to give your litter lots of love and attention during these early weeks. The result will be puppies who will make much better pets — with secure, loving personalities.

As the puppies learn how to use their bodies, they are also learning how to play with their littermates. Playing aids in developing their hunting skills, and helps them to develop healthy relationships with both you and their siblings.

All this movement and activity coincides with the early stages of weaning, which is not completed until they are approximately seven weeks old. Puppies may take a few days to get used to eating solids, finding it easier to continue feeding from their mother. Encourage them to make the switch as Mother will truly appreciate it. By now she will probably be rather skinny, and in need of extra food, and vitamin supplements.

Once the puppies are on solid foods, they will

need to be housebroken. You will have to make the decision whether to incorporate the intermediate step of paper training or to take them directly outside. If you choose the latter, you will need to monitor your puppies' water and food intake, and watch them with a hawk's eye. You must adhere to a regular schedule of taking them out for potty purposes. As soon as a puppy looks as if he is about to relieve himself, quickly take him outside. By your being both vigilant and consistent he will get the idea. Just be patient, and be sure to praise him profusely when he does what's expected of him.

If he does have an accident, clean the area thoroughly or the lingering scent will encourage him to use the same spot again. You may not detect an odor, but a dog's sense of smell is approximately twenty-eight times as acute as a human's. Odor neutralizers are available from pet stores.

C H O O S I N G   A   P U P P Y

Choosing a puppy should be one of life's happiest experiences – for both of you. In many instances the puppy, or puppies, will make the choice for you. You'll know you're meant only for each other when his or her big, soft puppy eyes meet yours.

What should you be looking for when choosing a puppy? Obviously, a lively, inquisitive temperament is important. A healthy puppy is full of vitality, and quickly responds to stimulus such as drumming fingers or verbal coaxing. Do remember, however, that puppies need a great deal of sleep. Do not be surprised if you don't see them awake for long. Try to visit several times, and also study the mother's character and behavior.

Of course, your future pet should have a clean, shiny coat, and bright eyes. Watery eyes, sneezing, and a dry nose are signs of infection, as is a generally undersized appearance. Unless you are prepared to spend time and money on the vet, it would be wise not to take a puppy in who appears to be in poor shape.

By keeping these basic rules in mind, you will enjoy and be successful at choosing your new companion. Once you have made the choice, he will be a dear friend and an important part of your life for many, many years to come.

IN THE BEGINNING

Life as a tiny puppy can be a little cramped but the closeness offers a real sense of security to the defenseless newborn. The average litter numbers from four to five puppies; however, eight or more are not uncommon. By squeezing tightly together they provide each other with warmth and the comfort of body contact. Potential dog owners should consider how many puppies were born to a litter (if the information is available). Dogs born to large litters may present more aggressive behavior traits than those that aren't, since as youngsters they may have had to compete with all of the other puppies for their mother's milk and for a space of their own.

STILL STAYING CLOSE TO MOM

If developing normally, the puppies should weigh five to seven times their birth weight by the time they are three to four weeks old. Their coordination should be better developed — they will not be as wobbly on their feet. Still, they depend on Mother for sustenance, and will not stray too far from her.

THE BABIES

Newborns are hardly bounding bundles of energy. Young infants greet the world not quite knowing which end is up. In fact, newborn puppies are both blind and deaf at birth. Their eyes open at around 10–14 days and do not focus properly for another seven. Hearing does not occur until 13–17 days, as their ear canals start to open. They are totally dependent upon their mothers for food, cleaning, and even for help with their bathroom skills.

◄ ► *By the time they are a month old puppies are quite a handful. By now they have graduated to running and rough-housing with their littermates. These bursts of activity are followed by frequent coma-like naps – just like human children. These quiet periods are appreciated by both their mother and you.*

BABIES NEED WARMTH

You would not dream of taking an infant out of the house on a cold winter's evening without bundling him up. The same applies to your puppy. You will need to provide him with warmth, just as his mother's body and the bodies of his littermates did when he was born. Do not assume that just because he has a fur coat he will be warm enough.

REAL FOOD

Much to the relief of Mom, puppies enjoy their first taste of real food at about three to five weeks of age. Learning to lap up food and liquids doesn't always come easily. Initially they may actually walk through their food, requiring you to wipe them off after meal time. Eventually they will get the hang of it, and will spend less and less time at their mother's nipples.

EASY DOES IT

Your new puppy's energy may seem boundless but you must remember that he is still a baby. Exercise, in the form of walks and play, is important for a puppy's healthy development. In fact, sufficient exercise will prevent many behavior problems later on in life. The key, however, is moderation. Start your puppy's exercise regime slowly, taking him only on brief walks at first. Save the longer outings for when he gets a little older.

Young puppies need to bond with each other in order to develop healthy psychological attitudes. It's important for puppies to spend just the right amount of time with their littermates before they're separated. Puppies who are taken away too early are denied the opportunity to interact with other animals. As a result, they may end up attaching themselves too closely to their new human owners. They may grow into submissive adults or, even worse, become over-protective of their owners. Conversely, puppies who live with their littermates for too long could grow up to be over-assertive, having spent too much time rough-housing with their brothers and sisters. Although experts vary on what the optimum age for separation is, the minimum should be eight weeks and the absolute maximum 12 to 14 weeks of age. This should allow enough time for the puppy to socialize with other dogs in the litter while leaving enough young, impressionable time to adapt to a new life.

DOUBLE TROUBLE

▼ ▼ *As the weeks and months go by you may notice that littermates sometimes pair off, especially in larger litters. If you have enough room in your home and your heart, why not adopt such a pair? If your job means that you must spend many hours away from home each day, your "twins" will keep each other entertained. With loneliness a major problem for our "latch-key" pets, a pair of puppies can be the perfect solution.*

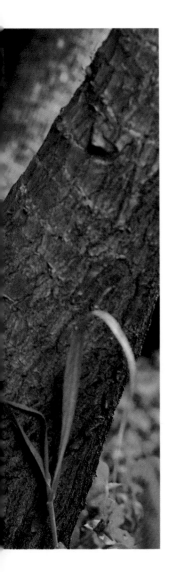

POKEY LITTLE PUPPY

Just like little children, puppies are incredibly inquisitive about the big world around them. They tend to poke their noses into everything — even where they do not belong. That's why it is so important to "puppy-proof" your home and yard. Get down on your hands and knees, and take a puppy's eye view of your home. Does your puppy have access to harmful household cleaners and chemicals? How about medications? Be sure to keep all of these out of his reach. The same goes for sharp items such as knives in the kitchen and rakes and hoes out in the yard.

Imagine how big the world must seem to a little puppy – it must be quite overwhelming. Luckily, puppies can take comfort by sharing strange, new experiences with their littermates. Take this little fellow's first encounter with snow early one morning. Can't you just imagine him saying, "Hey, guys! What is this cold, wet, white stuff anyway? I swear it wasn't here yesterday!"

◁ *Your puppy's first weeks on earth are spent socializing with his littermates, a period of interaction with others that is critical for your puppy's normal, healthy development. During this* time, he will run, play, and even fight with his brothers and sisters. You will be able to recognize the development of a pack hierarchy — some puppies will be natural leaders, others will be followers.

THE IMPORTANCE OF PLAY

△ *Playing aids your puppy in both his physical and psychological development. It hones his coordination, builds self-confidence, and channels his energy in a positive direction. By* providing your puppy with lots of toys — balls, rawhide bones, and so on you can encourage his activity. Remember, a tired puppy is less likely to get into trouble.

TEETHING

Puppies go through a teething stage just as human babies do. A puppy's first set of tiny, sharp teeth are temporary. At approximately four months of age, his permanent teeth cut through his gums causing swelling, inflammation and pain. The puppy will chew on virtually anything in order to relieve his pain. If your baby were teething, you would give him a frozen teething ring to soothe his gums. A rawhide bone that has been dipped in grave, or low-sodium broth, and frozen will serve the same purpose for your puppy.

THE
DOG AT PLAY

Dogs possess an inate playfulness that can bring a smile to the face of even the most serious individual. While puppies are particularly known for their playfulness, owners of mature dogs should not assume that their pets have no interest in play. Even adult dogs enjoy the addition of new toys to their collections, or a special game of tag with their owners.

THE IMPORTANCE OF PLAY

During the first weeks and months of life, play serves as a learning experience for puppies. Play teaches them how to relate to their littermates, their owners and the outside world. The socialization that results from their play experiences is absolutely critical for the puppies' normal development.

Regardless of age, regular play and exercise are vital for a dog's physical and psychological health and well-being. From a physical standpoint, lack of exercise generally results in obesity — unfortunately, a very common problem in canines, especially in older ones. From a psychological standpoint, lack of stimulation through exercise and play can lead to boredom, and result in a myriad of behavioral problems. In particularly severe cases, a lack of exercise can actually lead to depression in pets. It is, therefore, the owner's responsibility to ensure that his dog receives sufficient exercise, and play is an excellent means of accomplishing this.

THE PLAYFUL DOG

In addition to playing with their own kind, dogs love to play with their human companions. Some dogs even develop ways of signalling their desire to play with their owners. The most obvious is the dog who picks up her favorite toy in her mouth and prances over to her owner with that "come and get me" look in her eyes. Other dogs are more subtle. They may offer themselves to their owners in what is known as the play posture. This consists of the dog holding her tail high and wagging it, her front end down and her rear end up. She may play-bite, leap, nudge or nuzzle with her nose. She will often follow up this behavior with a backward jump, and quickly charge away from her owner. In essence, she is inviting her owner to chase her and enter into her world of play.

ENCOURAGING PLAY

Owners can do many things to encourage their dogs to play. Firstly, they can provide an environment conducive to activity. Providing lots of toys and an interesting yard goes a long way to encouraging their dogs' fitness. Spending time playing, walking or jogging with their dogs is another. Introducing a second dog into the house-

BATTLING BOREDOM

This little one looks as if she's thinking up ways to get into mischief. The number one cause of behavior problems in dogs is boredom. Chewing, excessive barking, hole digging, and general destructiveness can often be traced to a dog's lack of exercise and stimulation. This is especially common when dogs are left by themselves for extended periods of time with little to do. In fact, many dogs wind up in pounds and shelters due to such behavioral problems. These situations, however, can usually be easily resolved by encouraging them to play more and channel their energy positively.

CUTE BUT HAZARDOUS ESCAPADE

Puppies make an incredible transformation from helpless infants to mischief-makers in virtually no time at all. Within months those adorable little furballs reach the puppy equivalent of the "terrible two's." They become so absorbed in their play that they seem oblivious to the potential dangers around them. Take this little one, for example. Her frolicking with her toy has taken her under the leg of a chair. Should the chair be moved, the results could be painful. It's up to her owner to keep an eye on her to avoid such a mishap.

hold provides a playmate for a dog who is left alone for many hours while her owners are at work. Finally, if you are the owner of a senior dog, the addition of a new puppy into the household may be just the stimulation the older dog needs to keep hopping.

An excellent guideline for owners to determine what type and amount of activity is best suited for their dogs is to consider the dog's breed. Many of them were originally bred for specific purposes – for instance, Old English Sheep Dogs and Border Collies were bred for their alertness, stamina, and ability to herd. Dogs like these, therefore, generally require a lot of exercise, particularly a good run outdoors. Huskies, originally bred to pull heavy loads on sleds, also require a lot of exercise. While aquatic breeds, including Golden Retrievers, Labradors, Spaniels, Poodles and Newfoundlands, are renowned for their ability to swim, and their love of water. The insulated coats of these dogs, and certain physical adaptations such as the webbed feet and rudder-like tail of the Newfoundland, reflect their water-loving natures.

DANGEROUS TOYS

Pet shops are crammed with doggy toys. Many of them look great fun but you should check any toy over very carefully before purchase, just as you would if you were choosing something for a baby or small child. Can your dog chew or pull off any loose pieces from the toy? Can she swallow any part or all of it? If she can or might be able to, then don't buy the toy.

In fact, as you get to know each other better, you and your dog, or dogs, will soon learn to make your own toys and games. And with patience you should also be able to teach your dog some simple tricks. Most dogs get a great kick out of pleasing their owner in this way, but you should always encourage your pet with rewards – lots of hugs, kisses, and cuddles – to motivate her to repeat the game or trick.

TUG OF WAR

Whether played with other dogs or with people, one of the all time favorite canine games is "tug of war." It combines the dog's chewing/biting skills with the exertion of lots of muscle power. During the struggle, the dog may grunt and growl — but in a playful manner. The winner, who is inevitably the dog in dog–human competition, will trot off with her "prize" — parading it with all the pride of an Olympic gold medalist. One word of caution: do not permit your dog to play with household items you ultimately don't want her to play with. For instance, if you play tug-of-war with a sock, don't be surprised if your dog winds up playing with your best socks. As brilliant as she is, she cannot be expected to differentiate between one sock and another! Instead, it's better to use an item made specifically for play purposes — there are many toys available at pet shops solely made for games.

S P L A S H !

Many dogs love water and are excellent swimmers. Especially known for their affinity for water are Labradors, Poodles, Newfoundlands and, pictured here, Golden Retrievers and Spaniels. In fact, many of these breeds have physical adaptions that make them particularly suited for swimming. For many dogs, a lake, pond, ocean or even swimming pool is an open invitation to take a plunge. It's important, however, to remember that not all dogs know how to swim. Since fatal accidents can occur when curious dogs with no water skills fall in and panic, caring pet owners should always carefully supervise their dogs around water.

THE DOG AT PLAY

THE ILLUSTRATED DOG'S LIFE

WATER FETCH

Water fetch is the most common water sport for dogs. This game is especially popular with the hunting and sporting breeds since it incorporates their instinctive retrieving behavior with their love of water. In the beginning, it's very important that the owner choose a toy or object that floats — rubber balls are ideal. Newcomers to the game may be confused or upset when their favorite toy sinks out of sight. More seasoned players, like the Standard Poodle pictured here, can graduate to the more advanced game of diving fetch. In this game, the dog retrieves a sunken object by diving under the water. Note that the Standard Poodle's curly coat aids her buoyancy in the water.

POETRY IN MOTION

Several breeds of dog are known for their fleet footedness. Greyhounds, for instance, are legendary for their speed, and continue to be raced for sport in many countries. Other breeds known for their swiftness include the Whippet, Saluki, Borzoi and, pictured here, Afghans. Note the grace with which these long-legged, streamlined beauties run. Their feet don't seem to touch the ground! Used centuries ago to hunt swift gazelles, antelopes, wolves and foxes in the cold, rugged climate of exotic Afghanistan, today's Afghans still retain their long, silky coats and that endless desire to run and run.

TOYS ARE NOT JUST FOR KIDS

Playing with toys is not simply puppy stuff. No matter what her age, a dog can get immense enjoyment from playing with toys. Older dogs will especially benefit from the cardiovascular and muscular workout they get while playing. Many owners simply assume that older dogs have no interest in playing, and consequently do not buy new toys for their four-footed best friends. In reality, nothing could be further from the truth! Sprawled on her back, ball between her paws, you can see that, although full-grown, this one's obviously enjoying herself. In fact, doesn't she look like she's smiling?

GOOD CATCH!

 *Playing Frisbee is the logical extension of playing catch or fetch. It combines several favorite canine activities — leaping, dashing, and holding an object while running so it's no wonder our dogs delight in this game! Aside from being fun, the sport offers many benefits; the dogs'*

hearts, lungs, and muscles get a real aerobic workout. It's the ideal way for our pets to channel all that pent-up energy productively and, because you play it with your pet, you also enjoy the benefits of healthy exercise.

STEEPLE CHASE

While not as adept at jumping as cats, dogs still can be quite graceful and skillful when leaping over fences, hedges, and a variety of other obstacles. Owners of dogs who habitually jump over fences and onto the neighbor's property know this to be a fact! Owners should intepret this to be their dog's way of telling them that their yard isn't nearly interesting enough. Owners can increase their yard's appeal, and encourage their dogs' activity by adding lots of toys, hanging an old tire from a tree to serve as a canine punching-bag, or creating their dog's own personal obstacle course.

MAKING HER OWN FUN

Owning two or more dogs is the ideal situation since you are providing them with live-in playmates. This is especially true if you are gone from home for long periods at a time. However, dogs — just like children — can be quite creative when it comes to playing by themselves. They have their own ways of making their own fun. Regardless of their ages, even something as simple as a snowfall can bring out their inate playfulness. This one is having a fine old time rolling herself in the cold, new-fallen snow.

PERFECT PLAYMATES

There is no more heart warming a sight as a child and his dog sharing playtime together. Most adults do not have the time nor the energy to keep up with the frantic pace of either a young dog or a young child, but by contributing a ball for a game of catch, parents create the perfect way to channel both youngsters' seemingly boundless energies. In addition to helping develop a loving relationship between the child and pet that will last a lifetime, this activity is bound to leave both players exhausted after a while. And after all, a napping dog or child is much less likely to get into mischief!

THE
DOG IN A
MAN'S WORLD

Although dogs have been living with man for thousands of years, always remember that when you share your home with a dog you have taken him into your world. While amongst the most adaptable of creatures, dogs' natural curiosity and playfulness can get them into serious trouble in a man's world. It is, therefore, up to you not to take any unnecessary risks with their safety or sense of security.

DANGERS IN THE HOME

The word "home" generally conjures up the image of a happy, safe, secure place for family and family pets. Unfortunately, statistics reveal a different story. In fact, most accidents that happen to people happen in their own homes. Sadly, the same is often true for our pets. In order to make your home a secure refuge for both your family and your dogs, it is necessary for you to take steps to make sure that it is so.

Such commonplace actions as loading the washing machine or tumble dryer, opening and closing the refrigerator, closet doors or windows are likely to spark your dogs' curiosity. Dogs, particularly puppies, are interested in just about everything around them and that could lead them into some dangerous situations. It's important, therefore, to always look carefully when opening or closing anything in your home. If you are in a hurry, or distracted, you may easily trap your pet somewhere without knowing it. To decrease the chances of this occurring, you should always know where your dog is. Take special care to see where he is before leaving the house.

Around the house and yard, take the same precautions with your dogs as you would if you had small children. Household chemicals – including bleach, disinfectant, and some detergents – can be deadly. Keep these items safely locked up, or put away. And, by all means, keep family members' medications out of reach.

Something as seemingly innocuous as an unsecured garbage pail can be a hazard if your dog can raid it. Small bones lodged in your pet's throat or improperly disposed of chemicals can have tragic results. The same holds true for fireplaces and wood-burning stoves. Many a coat and paw have been singed by stray embers, so be sure to use a good screen and never leave your dogs unsupervised while the fire is going or the coals are hot. The same rules apply to outdoor barbeque grills. These tend to be great temptations for our pets because of the delicious odors that emanate as you grill steaks, hamburgers, and other foods.

Hazards abound in the yard and the garage, too. Potentially harmful chemicals include pesticides, some types of weedkiller, paint stripper, and sweet-tasting automobile anti-freeze. Even some fertilizers spread on your lawn can pose a threat to your dogs and other neighborhood animals, and there are also certain plants that are poisonous to dogs. If you are unsure as to the safety of the flora and fauna in your yard, consult with your local nursery or garden center. If your dog shows any sign of having been poisoned, get him to the veterinarian immediately.

Finally, keep tools and gardening implements out of reach. Sharp points and razor-sharp edges could do serious damage to your dog.

MOVING HOUSE

Moving house is as stressful for animals as it is for you, but careful planning will help to soften the trauma. Involve your dog in the packing-up as much as possible. Don't lock him away, but keep him among the family so he can see what is going on. Keep to his normal routine as much as possible, maintaining his schedule of walks and keeping his food dish in its normal place.

If at all possible, take your dog to the new home before moving day. Let him sniff around and become familiar with his soon-to-be new home, both inside and out. By walking with him and talking to him in a positive manner as he investigates, you will convey a sense of security. If you express anxiety or apprehension, he will almost certainly be quick to pick up on it.

If a "preview" of his new home is out of the question, on moving day follow the procedure in the preceding paragraph. No matter how busy you may be with the movers and the boxes, it's important to take the time to introduce your dog to his new surroundings. Place his food and water in an area similar to where it had been at the old premises. Provide him with something to play with. Give him lots of extra hugs for reassurance, and all this will help him to feel settled.

It is advisable to keep a close watch on your dog, especially when he is outside, for a few days after moving. It will often take a few days or weeks for him to become accustomed to his new environment. Keep to his routine as closely as you can, and make sure he has his new address on his collar.

GOING AWAY

Careful planning is also the key to leaving your dog successfully while you go away on vacation or business. By far the best arrangement is usually to keep the dog in his own home and pay a dog sitter, or persuade a dog-loving friend, to come in to feed, walk and exercise your pet. Dogs are territorial by nature, and the familiar smells and sound of your home help cushion your pet against the strain of being left alone.

If you can't get someone to dog sit for you, give your pet to a dog-loving friend to look after, or board him in a commercially run kennel. But do check it out beforehand, and if possible, choose one that is personally recommended.

DOGS AND CHILDREN

Often, when a couple does decide to start a family, they are apprehensive about their dog's reaction to the arrival of the new baby.

You should acclimate your dog to the new baby before its arrival. Do so by bringing home such common baby items and scents as baby powder, diapers, and baby oil weeks before the blessed event. Let your dog become familiar with the sounds a baby makes by playing a recording of a baby's cries and gurgles. Play-act by holding a baby doll and cooing over it. And, of course, while you're doing all this, continue to give your dog the same amount of attention and affection as he is used to.

When mother arrives home after her hospital stay, she should have father hold the baby while she enters the house alone. The dog will be excited to have her back, and deserves her undivided attention. Once the dog has settled down, father can enter the house with the new arrival. Of course, family and friends will want to visit the baby. By requiring them to fuss over your dog first, maybe even giving him a toy or rawhide bone as a present, he will not feel left out. In fact, he may think that the arrival of the new baby is the best thing that ever happened to him!

A NOBLE TRADITION

During the era of horse-drawn transport, the Dalmatian's love for accompanying horses on the road made him a fixture in stables and fire stations — earning him the nicknames "Coach Dog" and "Fire House Dog." Although motorized equipment replaces the horses today, the Dalmatian remains a mascot in many fire departments.

LATCHKEY DOGS

The advent of two-income households has created a new type of dog — the "shut-in" who's left on his own alone at home for many hours at a time, day in and day out. How do our dogs cope in this situation? Many of them spend the bulk of their days sleeping the hours away until their owners return home. Some are just plain bored and get into mischief just to while away the time — rummaging through the garbage pail, chewing on the furniture or digging holes in the carpeting. Others just can't cope with the loneliness and anxiety of being separated from their loved ones. They spend their days barking and destroying the house as they search in vain for their owners. Sometimes all a suffering latchkey pet that gets along well with other animals needs is another dog in the household. They will enjoy each other's company and feel secure knowing someone else is at home with them at all times.

ENVIRONMENTAL SAFETY

When you take a dog into your world, you are taking on responsibilities similar to those of raising a small child. In fact, it's necessary to take many of the same precautions with your pet as you would with a child. For instance, as soon as a child is able to speak and comprehend, parents teach him his name and his address. This information is essential should the child become separated from his parents. The same is true for your dog. Since we've not yet met a dog who can tell us his name and who his owners are, it's important that he wears the proper identification tags. It is also necessary to take the same precautions with your pets as you would with children when it comes to the application of pesticides, weedkillers and fertilizers to the lawn. Always follow the manufacturers' recommended rates and directions. If the manufacturer warns you to keep children off the lawn for a specified period of time after the application of such a product, the same rules apply to pets, as well.

ADAPTING TO A MAN'S WORLD

It's important to take your dog's needs into consideration at all times. While you can reach for a can of soda or a glass of water on a hot summer's day to quench your thirst, your canine comrade cannot. Instead, it is up to you to anticipate his needs. If you're taking him on an outing on a warm day, and you are unsure as to whether water is available for him, be sure to bring your own from home, plus a bowl for him to drink out of. This is a particularly good idea if you and your pet are vacationing together. After all, water varies from area to area, and strange water might lead to digestive upsets. Keeping this little fellow's long ears dry while he drinks presents a real challenge!

DOGGY MAKEOVER

Everybody deserves a little pick-me-up once in a while, including our dogs. Your dog will enjoy a good shampoo and conditioning, a hair styling, blow dry and pedicure, too. Not only will he look and smell better, but a makeover will make him feel better both physically and emotionally. While it's best to get your dog used to bathtime when he's young, dogs of any age can become accustomed to being bathed. Introduce your dog to bathtime gradually — start by getting your pet used to being in a tub or sink without any water. Be sure that he's wearing his collar so that you have something to hold onto, and place a non-skid mat under him for traction. You may want to place his favorite toy in the tub to encourage him. Once he's become adjusted to the tub, you can add a little warm (not hot) water — just enough to wet his paws. You may want to practice this a few times until he seems comfortable. With a little time and patience, you'll be scrubbing away in no time at all.

If your dog wants to join you for a dip in the pool, be sure to take the same precautions as you would with a small child. First and foremost, never let him go into the water unsupervised – no matter how good a swimmer he is. Do not let him be exposed to the sun's strong reflected rays for an extended period of time. Too many rays could damage his eyes, and, in some instances, over-exposure could lead to heat stroke. Also keep in mind that constant exposure to water and sun is very drying to your pet's coat and skin. This is particularly true of chlorinated pool water and ocean water, in which chemicals and salt can remove the vital oils and moisture from his coat. The results can be dry hair, itchy skin, and a bleached coat. To help counteract these effects, it's a good idea to rinse your dog with fresh water after he's gone for a swim in chlorinated or salt water. It appears that this fellow has figured out a way to avoid at least some of these problems!

CANINE CANOEING

No matter how good a swimmer your dog may be, it's important to get him a canine live-preserver if you intend to take him out boating with you. Before actually going out on the water, you should get him accustomed to wearing it. Some dogs accept wearing a life-preserver readily, while others may have to be introduced to it gradually — wearing it for short periods of time at first until they can tolerate it for longer periods of time. Once you take your dog out on the boat, be sure you provide him with a shaded area. Even on a cloudy day, the sun's rays are intensified by their reflection on the water. You'll also need to provide your dog with some fresh, cool water to drink. Finally, take extra care if you plan to go fishing. Sharp fishhooks lodged in delicate paws can be very painful!

As every dog owner knows, each dog has its own individual personality. Just as with people, dogs' personalities are the result of their upbringing, and the sum total of their life experiences. One cannot and should not generalize about a given breed. None the less, people cannot resist projecting their own feelings onto their canine companions. How many times have you heard a proud owner say, "Isn't he cute?" while cooing over what appears to be a vicious-looking dog! It has also been observed that dogs often take on the personalities and looks of their owners — for instance, so-called "he men" are often seen in the company of "macho" dogs like Dobermans or Rottweilers.

Take this tough-looking fellow in the Fedora. If dogs look like their owners and vice versa, can't you just imagine his owner as a fat, jowly-looking underworld figure who also wears a Fedora and smokes a big cigar?

THE FASHIONABLE HOUND

A multi-million dollar industry has mushroomed to cater specifically to the whims of pampered dogs and their owners. The well-groomed dog can splash out on canine shampoos, coat conditioners, detanglers, whiteners, brighteners, and even perfumes, breath fresheners, and deodorants. The fashion-conscious dog — or rather owner — can choose from designer collars, leashes, harnesses, jeans, T-shirts, hats, footwear, eyewear, backpacks, and jewelry. There are even doggy bridal gowns, tuxedos, and Halloween costumes! And for those owners who want to be perfectly coordinated when stepping out with their pets, the ultimate is matching outfits for themselves and their dog.

A REAL PARTY ANIMAL

Did you know that dogs can go through a mid-life crisis just like some middle-aged humans? Once the novelty of being the new pet in the family has worn off — no more puppy-cuteness, no more excitement — our dogs often become taken for granted, and treated as just another piece of the furniture. If this scenario sounds familiar, then shame on you! Middle-aged dogs, like dogs of any age, need both physical and mental stimulation to remain in good health. People going through a mid-life crisis will often change their hair styles or hair color, or go out and buy a new outfit for themselves. Since your dog cannot go out and do this, he'll need a little help from you. Why not throw a party for him and his canine pals? Of course, be sure that you invite other dogs he gets along with. You and the other owners can have a nice visit while your dogs have a chance to socialize.

THE BEST OF
TIMES AND THE
WORST OF TIMES

Once you have made the decision to take a dog into your home, it is a lifelong commitment. If for some reason you are no longer able to care for him, it is your responsibility to find him another suitable, loving home. For a dog that is used to living in a comfortable home, the cold steel cages and cement floors of an animal shelter or the local pound are a traumatic experience. These institutions tend to be overcrowded and overburdened by the canine population explosion that has resulted from people not spaying and neutering their pets. In fact, many pounds and shelters destroy their animals if they are not adopted within a specified period of time. Sadly, older adult dogs are often the least adoptable and, therefore, more likely to be destroyed. Instead, run ads in your local newspaper, and carefully screen prospective adoptive families. After all, you chose to bring him into man's world.

TABLE MANNERS?

It's important to be extra
vigilant when leaving food
out — especially if it's
within your dog's reach. If
you don't keep a careful eye
on your canine, you may
wind up encountering a
scene similar to this one! As
cute as it may seem, your
pet is actually exposed to
many dangers. Table
settings featuring sharp
knives could slice tiny

paws. Bowls of hot soup
and pots of hot coffee could
cause painful burns if
knocked over. If the table
cloth is dragged off the
table, ceramic dishes and
glassware could come
crashing down on the
floor, and shatter into
dangerous, sharp pieces
around your pet. And any
leftover bones, if
swallowed, could lodge in

his throat with tragic
results. That's why it's
particularly important to
teach your best friend good
table manners.

BEGGING AT THE TABLE

To some people, a dog begging at the dinner table is an adorable nightly ritual. To others, particularly when guests are dining, it's an annoying and embarassing habit. On one hand, how can one resist handing over a tasty morsel — especially when those big eyes stare at you, and those tiny little paws are outstretched beseechingly? On the other hand, who can tolerate the whining, whimpering and begging? If your dog steals food, begs, or jumps on someone seated at the dinner table it is most likely due to a lack of discipline. You'll need to teach him some table manners. Rather than putting him away in another room while you dine, try feeding him his own dinner in his own bowl while you eat yours. If this doesn't work, it may be necessary for you to command him to lie down and stay, with his collar and lead on, while you dine.

STRUGGLING IN A MAN'S WORLD

Sadly, every year thousands upon thousands of dogs are abandoned by the very people who took them in in the first place. The reasons are varied — some people simply move, and choose not to take the family pet with them. Others have experienced some type of behavioral problem with their dog, and choose to turn the animal loose rather than correct the problem. (Ironically, the majority of canine behavior problems are actually created by the owners' ignorance, and are usually easily corrected.) Numerous other dogs become lost and are never reunited with their owners because they lack proper identification tags. Man's world is no place for a dog to wander. Automotive and truck traffic, railroad crossings, encounters with other animals, lack of food, and the elements are all sure to shorten his life span.

GROWING UP TOGETHER

Although raising a toddler or a puppy is a handful unto itself, raising both at the same time is really not much more difficult. After all, many of the safety precautions one takes for a child are also taken for a puppy. For instance, child-proofing a home — keeping chemicals, cleaning preparations, and other harmful products out of a child's reach — is identical to that of puppy-proofing. And researchers have recently discovered something that every dog owner has always known — children and pets are an unbeatable combination.

Studies now show that children who are raised with pets are better adjusted than those who are not.

MAN'S WORLD FROM A DOG'S EYE VIEW

Since you have taken a dog into your world, it's important to take his needs into consideration. Imagine how overwhelming man's world appears from his perspective. People tower over him like threatening giants. Annoying as it may be, it's no wonder many dogs have a tendency to jump on us. After all, it's their only means of making eye contact with us. That's why it is so important that we get down on our hand and knees — on their level. Perhaps that's another reason why children and dogs have such a special relationship. Not only do they share the bond of unconditional non-demanding love; they also share the common experience of living as tiny beings in a very big world.

COMPANIONSHIP IN WORK AND PLAY

No matter what we are doing, our dogs love to be with us. Children, in particular, develop strong bonds with their pets, and often become inseparable. Many four-footed best friends eagerly anticipate the end of the day — when their human brothers and sisters return from school. Whether they play, or accompany their two-footed best friends on their chores or afterschool jobs, the end of the school day is enjoyed as much by our pets as our children. In fact, it is not at all uncommon for dogs to go through a form of depression when their human siblings move away from home and off to college. Similar to the "empty nest" syndrome that parents experience when the children grow up and leave the household, dogs feel their absence, too. By giving your dog extra love and attention — maybe even another pet playmate — you can help make the transition easier.

THE
PHYSICAL DOG

Most dogs have a complete repertoire of verbal vocalizations that serve as a means of communication with the animals and people around them. Just as, if not even more, important are the non-verbal ways our dogs express themselves – through their body language.

CANINE BODY LANGUAGE

Dogs rely on their observations of the body language of other dogs and animals to gather information, and to communicate. These "readings" enable them to determine what the other's intentions are, and whether the stranger is friend or foe. Additionally, their own body language serves to communicate to fellow dogs what's on their minds. That is why the way a dog carries his or her body is no accident. The dog is telling us something. As owners, we can increase our understanding of our canine companions if we simply take the time to learn to translate this body language. And studying our pets' body language when they're well features an additional advantage – we'll quickly be able to recognize when they're feeling out of sorts.

THE EYES

Bright, fully opened eyes indicate that the dog is awake and alert. But if her eyes are opened so widely that the whites of her eyes are exposed, it may mean that the animal is alarmed and very fearful. Fearful and submissive dogs will often avoid making eye contact with those they feel subordinate to. Conversely, aggressive dogs will often stare challengingly at their perceived adversary.

Half-closed eyes indicate that a dog is relaxed, and somewhere between being awake and asleep. If she happens to be on your lap, it means she trusts you to some degree. By closing her eyes, actually nodding off in your presence, your pet is giving you her ultimate vote of confidence and trust. Finally, when a dog is not feeling well, the eyes will often reflect this fact. Their usual sparkle may be replaced with a marked dullness.

THE EARS

Ears indicate a dog's mood and purpose. Because they are so apparent, ears are generally an excel-

READY, WILLING AND ABLE

This German shepherd epitomizes total canine confidence. Her bright eyes sparkle as she scans her surroundings. She holds her tail erect, like a proud flag waving in the wind and her pricked ears demonstrate her keen alertness. Even the fluidity of her movement seems to say, "I'm in control." Her proud bearing conveys her intelligence, eagerness to please, and the fact that there's nothing you can ask of her that she won't do.

Dogs come in a myriad of shapes and sizes, and their coats come in just as many varieties. This tiny creature, a Chinese Crested, has no coat! Except for the flowing crest of silky hair crowning her head, and a plume on her tail, her entire body is covered by soft, smooth skin. Chameleon-like, her skin changes color with the seasons — darker tones in summer, lighter in winter.

lent barometer of canine body language — the only exceptions are the cropped ears of breeds such as Great Danes and Boxers. Ear cropping, the intentional trimming of the ears, results in the ears being permanently erect. Still performed in the United States, this practice is outlawed in the United Kingdom for humanitarian reasons.

Relaxed but normally alert ears will move a little, and change direction as they pick up the sounds around them. The ears on submissive and fearful dogs are usually pulled back, lying flat against the head, and serve as signals to other animals that their owner doesn't want a confrontation. The ears on an aggressive dog are usually out of their normal position but not quite flat against the head. They are often rotated somewhat to the front so that a portion of the back of the ear is almost facing forward. These ears say, "I'm ready for whatever comes my way." Ear twitching can occur with any emotional extreme, including delight, submission, or aggression. Finally, when your pet isn't feeling well, she will often pull back her ears in various positions and degrees depending on the amount of pain and physical upset she is experiencing.

THE TAIL

Here, again, the tail is an excellent guide — unless it has been docked. When a dog is relaxed, her tail simply hangs in a casual manner. It is neither up nor down, nor does it move very much. A wagging tail is often, but not always, a sign of happiness and positive excitement. It can also indicate that a dog is nervous or anxious. Similarly, a tail that thumps, or swings from side to side, can be a sign to watch out for. The faster and harder a dog moves or thumps her tail, the greater the degree of anxiety and/or aggression she is experiencing. To determine if this tail movement is indicative of distress rather than delight, it is necessary to take into consideration the rest of the dog's body. Watch for ears flattened against the head or rotated forward. Another warning sign you must watch for is bristling fur, particularly on the dog's back and neck. An aggressive dog will actually become measurably larger because the hair on her body is raised, giving her a puffed-up appearance. Aggressive dogs also arch their necks and stiffen their legs in preparation to springing into action. If this occurs, watch out for an attack!

Submissive and fearful dogs usually hold their tails low or between their legs. Here again, it is necessary to view the dog's body in its totality in order to draw the proper conclusion. For instance, a submissive dog will often assume a crouching position, then roll over onto her side, displaying her flank. In essence she is saying, "I surrender. I recognize that you're in charge and I have no intentions of challenging you." In contrast, a fearful dog can pose a threat. Generally speaking, fearful dogs are very unpredictable and may bite solely out of fear. Finally, if a dog holds her tail low or between her legs, she may be indicating discomfort due to pain or illness.

Unlike a "smiling" canine whose lips are slightly drawn back exposing her incisors, the way the lips are drawn back in aggression is much more pronounced. An aggressive dog will draw her lips back further, often exposing her pointed canine teeth. If experiencing "fearful aggression," the dog will emit a constant low growl, snarl or bark as a warning to the perceived threat. Her whole body will be tense, with her back legs held ready for rapid movement. Her tail will be held down and rigid, and her ears will be laid back. Often the hair down the middle of her back will stand on end, giving her a larger appearance . In the case of "dominant aggression," rather than simply warning off what she perceives as a threat, the dog will actually advance confidently with her tail and ears held high towards it.

DO DOGS SMILE?

Dogs are blessed with facial muscles that enable them to make an eloquent array of facial expressions. For instance, their lips can be curled back to expose their teeth. Interestingly enough, baring the teeth is not always a sign of aggression. Some dogs seem almost to laugh and, when very pleased, their lips draw back to expose their incisors. In fact, many Doberman owners have mistaken their dogs' smiling for aggression. If you have any doubt as to whether dogs smile, just take a look at these three Samoyeds. Now you know why they're alternately refered to as the "smiling dogs of the North!"

I SURRENDER

Confronted by three other canines, the black dog pictured here has adopted the classic submissive position – dogdom's equivalent of raising the white flag of surrender. This display of subordination begins with the dog lowering herself into a crouch. She then rolls over, displaying her flank, and raises one of her hind legs. Dogs assuming the submissive position will often fold back their ears close to their heads, and avoid making direct eye contact with their aggressors. By volunteering this posture, dogs transmit one of the most powerful signals in canine body language. In essence, this animal is acknowledging the dominance of the others.

LET'S PLAY

One of the cutest exhibitions of canine body language is the play-bow. During this special invitation to play, the dog will lower the front half of her body, with her chest nearly touching the ground. She'll keep her rear end raised, her tail held high and wagging. She may give little yips, barks, and non-threatening growls — as if to say, "Come on, let's play!" She may also play-bite, leap and nudge or nuzzle her intended playmate with her nose. This is usually followed with a backward jump, and a quick charge away from her companion — as if to provoke a chase. If her companion responds, a harmless chase, game of tag, or play-fight will ensue. While this behavior is usually directed towards people and other animals, this little gal proves that anything that moves is pretty fair game!

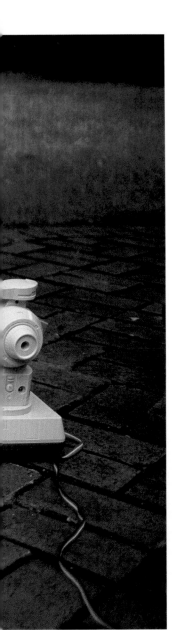

ON THE SCENT

△ The Bloodhound is renowned for her highly developed sense of smell. Although virtually all dogs are capable of detecting odors that are imperceptible to us, the Bloodhound's scenting ability is so acute that she is reputed to be able to follow a human's trail after a single exposure to some object the person has worn or handled. This ability is assisted, in part, by the folds of skin on the Bloodhound's face that give that characteristically wrinkled look. It is believed that these folds help "hold" the scent of the trail close to the dog's face. The long, floppy ears are believed to have been deliberately bred in to ensure that she concentrates on the scent and is not distracted by irrelevant sounds around her.

GENTLE GIANT

With a powerful, commanding appearance, the Irish Wolfhound is one of the largest dogs on earth. Despite their great size, it's amazing how cautiously they manage their extraordinary physical power. As the name suggests, this majestic dog was originally used to hunt wolves, plus elk and other large game in the British Isles — their powerful jaws, impressive muscular structure, and long legs made them highly suited for these fast-paced, strenuous sports. Hunting almost entirely on the basis of vision, and having a great sensitivity to seeing movement in the distance, the Irish Wolfhound is classified as a "sight hound" or "gaze hound."

WHAT WAS THAT?

This little one's expression seems to say, "Pardon me. What did you say? Would you kindly repeat it?" Here, again, a dog's facial muscles come into play. Some dogs are capable of raising their eyelids, brows, and ears when suprised or, as in this case quizzical. The cocking of her head to one side exaggerates this dog's questioning look. It's as if she's trying her best to understand. Also note the pronounced whiskers on her muzzle. Called "vibrissae," they are much more sensitive than the other hairs on her body. She depends on them to help guide her through narrow spaces at night, when darkness limits visibility.

Most dogs are fairly vocal: in fact, even the barkless Basenji communicates through a series of yodeling chortles. In general, dogs can produce a full range of sounds — from whimpers, to rolling growls, to proper barks. Like people, dogs use their voices to express themselves, raising the pitch or volume of their bark to indicate frustration or express emotion. It is interesting to note that barking isn't necessarily a sign of aggression. It may simply be the dog's way of saying "Hurry up, come and play!" or "I'm happy to see you," rather than "One false move and I'll tear your throat out!" As always, it is important to consider the circumstances under which the dog is barking. Take this little gal, for instance. Is she reacting to someone at the door? Or is she letting her owner know it's time for a walk? While we can't be sure, her owner certainly can.

COOLING OFF

With the exception of their feet, dogs' skin does not feature efficient sweat glands. While humans can lose heat rapidly by extensive body sweating, dogs have to rely on another type of cooling mechanism to help regulate their body temperatures — panting. If a dog begins to overheat, she simply opens her mouth, lets her tongue flop out, and begins rapid, heavy panting. While doing so, she'll moisten her tongue repeatedly in order to speed up the evaporation process. Because an overheated dog will drink more than usual to maintain a supply of liquid to her tongue's surface, it's important to be sure that our dogs always have access to water. Owners should also be sure to provide them with adequate shade — particularly during the hot summer months. Failure to do so could result in your dog suffering from potentially fatal heat stroke.

THE DOG
AS PREDATOR

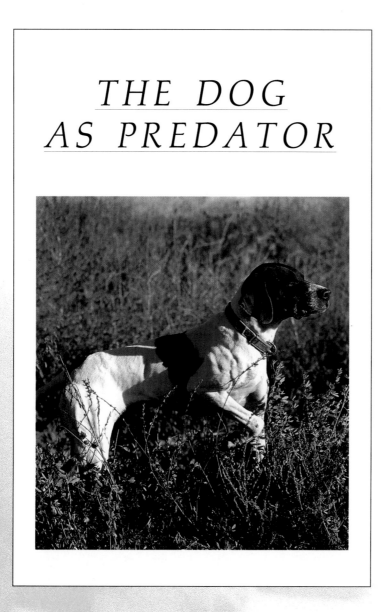

The first canines were hunters out of sheer necessity. Dogs were beasts of prey – their very survival depended on their hunting abilities. Thousands of years later, virtually all our dogs still display some degree of their ancestors' hunting instincts. It may be hard to believe that sweet Spotty, your precious little terrier, has predatory instincts, but just watch him as he stalks that unsuspecting butterfly! And if you don't believe that the instinct is inborn, simply watch a litter of tiny puppies as they pounce on one another during playtime.

HUNTING – A SYMBIOTIC RELATIONSHIP

The earliest cave paintings depict dogs as man's companions. Early man learned to rely on the hunting prowess of his dogs to provide him with food. After all, dogs possessed keen visual and olfactory senses, speed, and powerful jaws that enabled them to crush bones. Humans, in contrast, possessed manual dexterity, the ability to make weapons, and the ability to plan ahead. By combining their strengths and abilities, a wonderfully practical relationship developed. This mutually beneficial alliance yielded a more effective way to hunt – resulting in more food for both people and their dogs.

This successful alliance has lasted down through the ages. Even when sheep-herding and cattle-raising became established, thereby virtually eliminating the need to hunt for food for survival, man and his dogs continued to chase game. In some cases it persisted as a means of protecting these very herds from canine predators such as wolves, coyotes, and dingoes. However, as civilization progressed, this activity evolved into a favorite sport of mankind. The hunt became a social event, accompanied by much pomp and ceremony. Even today, this special alliance between humans and dogs continues with great pageantry in the sport of fox hunting.

SIGHT AND SCENT HOUNDS

Dogs are assets to hunters for practically every species of game, and people have bred them to take advantage of their particular abilities. Hunting dogs fall into one of two different classes of hunting – sight or scent. Scent hounds locate their quarry through body odor picked up by their keenly sensitive noses. They track their game, for hours if necessary, crossing fields, streams, thickets and forests. Scent hounds usually bark (or "give tongue") as they pursue their quarry, finally bringing it to bay on the ground or above them in a tree.

Sight hounds, as their name indicates, rely on their keen visual senses to spot their prey. Sight hounds were, and still are, important hunting companions in the plains and deserts of Africa and Asia. The air in these areas is hot and dry – not favorable conditions for scenting, but with very limited vegetation to obscure the view, it is ideal terrain for dogs who hunt by sight. Many of the sight hound breeds – Greyhounds, Afghans, Salukis and Borzoi, for example – are extremely fleet-footed as well. After sighting their prey, these streamlined canines can run at the great speeds needed to capture their quarry.

LUPINE ANCESTRY

No matter what breed of hunting dog we observe, we can easily recognize similarities between the dog's behavior and the behavior of its ancestor – the wolf. Many of our dogs today demonstrate behavior that can be traced directly back to the way wolves hunt in the wild. Take the Pointer, for example. Hunting game by scent, the Pointer assumes a frozen, statue-like stance when he comes upon his prey – it appears quite contrived but, actually, it is quite natural, and can be observed in the Pointer's lupine ancestors. Wolves in the wild perform a similar pause when they first scent their prey. Stopping dead in their tracks and pointing themselves rigidly in the direction of their quarry, leaders of the pack alert other pack members to the location of their prey. Humans have simply modified this natural pausing behavior by training Pointers to prolong this stance until released by the hunter.

Setters, another favorite breed of hunters, will get close to the ground and assume a low crouching position when they come upon their prey. By "setting" – a variation of the word "sitting" – and

The Pygmies of the Congo rely on the Basenji to point, retrieve, scent, and drive game into their waiting nets. They particularly appreciate him, for he stalks the vicious reed rats that plague their tribal villages. Often referred to as "the barkless dog," the Basenji is of special value for hunting small game since silence is a prerequisite for success. He communicates in a soft, yodeling chortle, and is fastidious about his hygiene – cleaning himself in cat-like fashion.

fixing their gaze in the direction of their quarry, they alert their hunting companions. Here, again, the action of the setter is reminiscent of the wolf's behavior in the wild. During the hunt, wolves often employ a similar ambushing technique during which one wolf will circle round, and then lie hidden, waiting for the prey to be driven in its direction.

Retrievers rush after fallen prey, even entering cold marshes and icy lakes to do so. They bring their quarry back to their human hunting companions without consuming it themselves. This is similar to wolves in the wild who have been observed taking food back to the den for nursing she-wolves or for newly weaned cubs. The behavior of retrievers is probably simply an adaptation of this selfless lupine food-sharing tendency.

Finally, the skills of herding dogs, who control sheep and cattle, can also be traced back to their carnivorous ancestors. Wolves can control and direct herds of wild animals in such a way as to make them vulnerable to attack. Working in unison, several wolves will separate a weaker member of the herd from the main body, and drive it into the direction of waiting pack members.

WOLVES HUNTING

Upon scenting their prey, the leading members of the wolf pack freeze in their tracks, and point themselves rigidly in the direction of the scent. The other members of the pack then follow suit, trying to catch the scent themselves. Once they have all fixated on the odor of the prey, they begin the next phase of their hunting operation. If they happen upon a herd of grazing animals, they will attempt to isolate one of the animals from the herd.

Generally speaking, the unlucky victim is often a weaker member of the herd — young, ill, or somehow disabled. Once the prey is separated from the safety of the herd, one wolf will make a decoy attack from the front, attempting to seize the animal's nose. This frontal attack merely serves to distract the victim. Another wolf will launch a more serious attack from the rear. Ultimately, it is this second attack that brings down the animal.

CALL OF THE WILD

Observation of wolves in the wild reveals that there are generally two reasons for howling. First, it serves as a rallying cry, announcing the intention to hunt. Hence, wolves howl most in the early evening before departing on a group hunt, and in the early morning before setting off once again. Howling is also provoked when the pack is scattered. It serves to reunite the social unit. Since it is rare for our domestic dogs to go off hunting on their own, they tend to bark more than howl. In general, the only time that a domestic dog howls is when he is forcibly shut away from his pack — the family. Then he performs a mournful, heart-wrenching howl of loneliness. Whether this type of howling is performed by wolves or by our domestic dogs, the message is the same: "I'm here . . . Where are you? . . . Come join me."

COMBINED SKILLS

The German Shorthaired Pointer possesses a winning combination of hunting skills — pointing and retrieving. No wonder he is a favorite all-purpose gundog in his native country and throughout the world. The German Shorthaired Pointer is just as comfortable hunting wildfowl as he is rabbits, possum and raccoon. Equally adept at working in open fields, marshes, woods or mountains, he follows wild game by scent. Once he comes upon his quarry, he instinctively assumes the rigid stance that is his trademark — the "point." But the German Shorthaired Pointer's hunting tasks do not end here. Once the hunter has hit his mark, this versatile dog will retrieve the quarry — even braving rough, icy waters to do so.

Thousands of years ago, hunters realized that certain quarry were simply too fast, too smart or too out of reach for them to capture. They therefore enlisted the assistance of their canine companions to get the job done. Today, the result of this alliance is reflected by a myriad of canine hunting breeds. People, realizing that different dogs possessed different abilities, bred them for specific hunting tasks. Take the Bluetick Coonhound for example. Possessing an inbred "treeing" instinct, he is perfectly suited for hunting raccoon, oppossum and other arboreal animals. He trails his quarry by scent — his nose to the ground in Bloodhound fashion. Once the game takes refuge up in a tree, he "gives voice" — barking to let his hunting companion know where their prey is cornered.

LYING IN WAIT

When it comes to duck hunting, there is hardly a dog better suited for the challenge than the Labrador Retriever. Known for his scenting powers, love of water, and innate game-finding ability, his short, dense coat is water-repellant, and insulates him from the cold. He will lie silently by his hunting companion until their prey comes within range. Once a shot is fired, he will spring forward, swim to the fallen game, and fetch it. Prized for his "soft" mouth, the Labrador Retriever's jaws will not damage the game in his grip.

HOLDING POINT

A specialized breed of gundog, the Pointer hunts by scent. Upon detecting hidden prey, he freezes statue-like in his tracks. While holding "point", his neck is stretched forward, and his tail is held stiffly in a horizontal position. The most startling element of his pointing posture is the position in which he holds one front foot — up in midair as if caught in midstep. Standing completely still, the Pointer will hold this position seemingly forever. Only after the hunter has fired his gun at the prey does the Pointer release his point and resume tracking.

TALLY HO!

Riding to hounds, was not always considered a sport. Originally hunting foxes with large packs of hounds served the practical purpose of ridding sections of the countryside of an animal many farmers considered to be a threat to livestock and poultry. It evolved into a formal sport featuring hunters mounted on specially bred and trained horses, which follow as the hounds track the fox by scent across the countryside, over fences, ditches and streams.

LOOKS CAN BE DECEIVING

It may be hard to believe but these three adorable little fellows are actually representatives of a breed often referred to as African Lion Hounds, and are known to be fearless hunters of lions and other big game! Officially called Rhodesian Ridgebacks, they get their name from the peculiar line of black hair that runs the length of the spine. This line of hair grows in the opposite direction to the rest of the coat, creating a distinctive crest along the center of the back. In their native land, packs of Rhodesian Ridgebacks are used by hunters to track large quarry. The pack instil panic in their prey and drive it towards the hunter who finishes the job.

THE WILD DOGS OF AFRICA

Living in packs, Cape Hunting Dogs are skinny creatures with prominent ears and distinctive "tortoiseshell" markings. The yellow, white, and black speckles and blotches on their coats serve as camouflage as they stalk their prey on the African savannah. Hunting in packs of 15–20, Cape Hunting Dogs lie in wait among the tall grasses until they spot a solitary antelope or zebra. They then hurl themselves upon their victim, accompanying their attack with very sharp, harsh barking. Lacking the power of their relatives the wolves, they rely on their social hunting skills to bring down their prey.

SEMI DOMESTICATION

While despised by ranchers because of their propensity to kill sheep, dingoes are valued by the native tribes of Australia for that very hunting instinct. Tribesmen steal dingo pups from their mothers, and patiently rear them. When the young dingoes are grown, they are used to flush game from the thickets out into the open. This mutual hunting is, however, short-lived. Although dingoes willingly live and hunt with people, they never become totally attached to them. At the start of the mating season, they will leave the human families which have cared for them, and establish their own packs in the wild.

Smaller than a wolf but larger than a fox, the jackal is believed to have descended from wolves. The jackal is less powerful and has a less aggressive temperament than his lupine relatives. Lacking their savage defensive powers, he tends to be much more timid, and generally resorts to scavenging instead of hunting. The jackal's varied diet consists of fruit, insects, reptiles, amphibians, small mammals, and carrion.

However, if these sources of food become scarce, they will form packs to go hunting. As a result of their mutual efforts, jackals have been known to pull down large animals, including antelope and gazelle. All in all, the jackal is still chiefly known for being a scavenger. Serving effectively as Nature's "street cleaners," jackals are often tolerated by residents of some Asian and African cities for this very reason.

THE
SOCIABLE DOG

How sociable are dogs? The answer is "very." From the moment of birth, dogs find themselves thrust into a social situation. It is very rare for a bitch to produce only a single puppy, so newborn pups are immediately exposed to a multitude of siblings, and the litter quickly develops a "pecking order." You'll see it in the greedy little glutton who pushes all her littermates aside to fasten on the best nipple, and in the tiny runt who seems always to be the last to be fed. Soon every pup knows its place in the litter's pecking order — who it should defer to, and who it can boss about.

CANINE SOCIETY – THE PACK

Observation of dogs in nature — without the intervention of humans — also reveals the existence of a definite social hierarchy. Whether the pack is one of wild dogs on the African plains, or a gang of formerly domesticated strays who roam the local city park, you will immediately note the existence of a distinct social order.

The key member of the pack is its leader. The leader's role is to watch over, protect, guide, and maintain order among its fellow pack members. This position is usually held by the bravest, strongest and most alert of the animals. As the pack's very survival often depends on the abilities of its leader, the position generally goes to the dominant male animal. For the most part, the other pack members voluntarily submit to his leadership for the sake of their own preservation. Should the leader's abilities become impaired, thereby jeopardizing the pack's survival, the leader will be challenged by a stronger, healthier animal. These challenges take the form of physical confrontations, usually initiated by a younger male. The victor in each of these challenges earns the right to the leadership role.

DOGS AND MAN TODAY

Although dogs have been in human care for thousands of years, we should not assume that today's dogs have lost their natural instincts. For instance, the pack instinct definitely remains intact. Today's dogs view their human families as a pack, and their owners as pack leaders responsible for their protection and security. Humans share their food, share their den (the family home), go out patroling the territory together (walks around the property or neighborhood), and play together.

Another basic instinct that remains intact today is a dog's territorial instinct. Since prehistoric times, and continuing right on up to the present, dogs have protected the home and its occupants from both human and canine intruders. Considering people and other dogs as members of its own kind, a dog is naturally wary of — and sometimes actually aggressive toward — unfamiliar members of both these species. Even the most docile dog may demonstrate territorial aggression by barking, growling showing her teeth, and chasing what she perceives to be an intruder. This is particularly true when her owner is not present. In essence, in the absence of the pack leader, the dog takes over the role as protector of the pack's territory.

MOUNTING

Perhaps the most misunderstood form of canine social behavior is mounting. Many people make the mistake of assuming that mounting is strictly a form of sexual behavior. In other words, they believe that the only time this position is taken is when the male dog is about to finalize the canine mating ritual. This assumption is an erroneous one. While the male dog does indeed straddle the female from behind during canine coitus, you may observe male dogs attempting to mount other male dogs. On occasion you may even see bitches attempt to mount each other. No — this does not necessarily mean that the mounting dog is exhibiting homosexual tendencies. It is much more likely to be a demonstration of dominant behavior, a display of who's the boss. While we humans tend to view this behavior only in sexual terms, in the canine world it's viewed in terms of power.

You may be wondering, "Why does my dog attempt to mount my leg?" Or perhaps you've been both embarassed and annoyed when your dog suddenly chose to mount the leg of a guest in your home? Here, again, the answer is that it is more likely to be a demonstration of dominance than a demonstration of sexuality. This is particularly true if this amorous-looking display occurs on the leg of a visitor to your home. Take solace in knowing that the dog's territorial instinct is taking over, and simply attempting to show your guest who's in charge!

INTRODUCING NEW
FURRY AND FEATHERED
FAMILY MEMBERS

As we have seen, dogs maintain many deeply rooted basic instincts, including territorial protectiveness and dominance. It is, therefore, not surprising that people assume that it is difficult to introduce a new pet into a household with an existing dog. Unfortunately, this assumption is reinforced by such phrases as "You can't teach an old dog new tricks." With terrible visions of their dogs making *hors d'oeuvres* out of little kittens, and the cat scratching out their dog's eyes, it's no wonder that many owners hesitate to introduce a new pet!

Actually, nothing can be further from the truth. Our dogs' sociable nature enables them to live in harmony with other animals under the same roof. With a little time, planning and patience, dogs of any age can be taught to live happily with other members of the animal kingdom.

Puppyhood is the ideal time to introduce your dog to another animal. If done within the first three months of life, your puppy will most likely accept the other animal as a littermate or fellow pack member. Older dogs are generally accepting of young animals, too and seem to realize that the other animal is a baby, and not a threat. Of course, the introduction of any new animal to an existing pet should be done cautiously, with plenty of supervision. Even the most well-meaning adult dog could harm a young animal with rough play.

Finally, it is possible to introduce your older dog to an older animal. Unfortunately, the biggest mistake owners make is bringing home a new animal and plunking it down into the existing pet's space. How would you feel if suddenly, without any warning, a stranger moved into your home? Now, imagine how your dog would feel – yes, he'd feel just the same!

PROTECTIVE PAWS

Nestled between the protective paws of her Basset Hound buddy, this little hamster looks totally at ease. In fact, the look in her friend the Basset Hound's eyes seems to say, "Don't bother my little furry friend or you'll have to answer to me!" Ironically, because Basset Hounds are smaller and slower than many of the other hound breeds, they are often used to hunt rabbits and hares. These two are proof that, with a little time and a lot of patience, dogs can form an attachment with almost any member of the animal kingdom.

It's best to acclimate your existing pet to the idea of a new housemate before its actual arrival, ideally by introducing her to the newcomer on neutral territory. If this is not feasible, introduce her to the scent of the newcomer before its arrival, by bringing something containing the newcomer's scent into your home several days or weeks earlier.

Finally, when the new animal arrives at your home, your existing pet should never have to compete with her new roommate for your attention. No matter how tempting it is to fuss over the newest arrival, especially if it's a cute little puppy or a cuddly little kitten, give your existing pet the same (if not more) attention as before.

EARLY SOCIALIZATION

Puppies are literally born into a social situation, usually sharing their mother's attention with several littermates. Watch a litter of puppies, even for a short period of time, and you'll observe a distinct social order. You'll see individual puppies who exhibit natural leadership abilities, and less aggressive puppies who prefer to follow. And, of course, there's Mother to keep an eye on them all, to set an example, and to keep them in line. In essence, the litter is similar to a miniature pack. It serves as ideal preparation for the future — whether the pack society of dogs in the wild, or the family pack of the human household.

A key part of any puppy's early socialization is play fighting. Watch a litter of puppies and you'll observe them chasing and pouncing on each other during mock battles. These bouts serve as a sort of basic training — sharpening the puppies' predatory skills. During such play fights you may even observe them baring their teeth and nipping at their littermates while growling and yelping. While it's always prudent to supervise these fighting furballs, such mock battles generally sound a lot worse than they actually are. You might say their barks are a great deal worse than their bites! In fact, after the battle has ended, you may find the little "warriors" snuggled together for a much needed nap.

One of our dogs' strongest instincts is the territorial instinct — the desire to protect the pack's home and property. The mail carrier and the newsboy are often targets of this instinctive behavior. The very nature of their work actually serves to reinforce a dog's protective behavior. These perceived interlopers make brief visits — simply making deliveries, then quickly departing. The dog attributes their rapid departures to her warning them off by barking, growling, and challenging them — in other words, the dog believes it was her aggressive behavior that scared them and caused them to retreat. Having successfully protected her territory, the dog is encouraged to do the same the next time a stranger appears.

MEETING ON NEUTRAL TERRITORY

◀ While the ideal situation is to introduce two dogs as puppies and raise them together, dogs of any age can learn to coexist peacefully, if not happily. Since dogs have such strong territorial instincts, it is best to introduce them on "neutral territory" — at a park or a friend's home. By introducing them in an area where neither dog has formed an attachment, you can help bypass the aggression that sometimes accompanies the territorial instinct. Ideally, the future housemates should be introduced on neutral territory on several occasions. During each of these meetings, they should be wearing their collars and leads, and, of course, be carefully supervised.

THE MATING GAME

While the unneutered male dog is sexually ready throughout the year, the unspayed female experiences only two limited times when she is fertile. These estrus periods, referred to as heat, generally occur in the early spring and again in the fall. The canine mating ritual usually commences with nose-to-nose sniffing, occasionally accompanied with some ear-licking, followed by some mutual rump sniffing, after which the male will move to the bitch's side and rest his head on her back. When ready, the female swings her tail to one side, thus enabling the male to mount her. As it is instinctive for dogs to mate, it is imperative that owners of unspayed bitches supervise them during heat. Sadly, animal shelters are filled with unwanted puppies — a result of irresponsible owners not taking proper precautions.

GETTING TO KNOW YOU

Generally speaking, humans interact on the basis of sight and sound. When two people meet, they recognize each other by sight, and greet each other by saying "Hello." In contrast, dogs interact on the basis of scent. They rely on their extremely well-developed sense of smell to "size up" other dogs, unfamiliar surroundings, and even people. A perfect illustration of this is how a pair of dogs act when they encounter each other for the first time. They will immediately begin sniffing each other — their noses virtually touching. Next, the dogs will circle around each other while continuing to sniff. It is always wise for an owner to maintain a firm grip on his pet's lead when encountering a strange dog of unknown temperament.

FIGHTING LIKE CATS AND DOGS?

▶ It is true that cats often bring out a dog's natural predatory instinct. After all, cats are generally small, furry, and quick-moving — the perfect object of a chase! Fortunately, in most cases the chase is a harmless one — resulting only in some hissing and spitting from the cat. Occasionally, however, a cat may stand its ground, and the dog may wind up with a scratch on its nose. Interestingly enough, dogs can distinguish between one cat and another, and will live happily and peacefully with its own family's cat. The very same dog who chases the neighbor's cat or the local strays will often sleep nose-to-nose with her family's feline!

Here's proof that dogs can peacefully co-exist with other animals. Although face to face with a member of another species, neither dog pictured here is displaying any signs of aggression — no bared teeth,

no growling, no barking. In fact, they both look rather relaxed! This is due in part to the fact that their companions are young — a chick and a piglet. It is believed that young animals emit a scent that our dogs

interpret as "I'm a baby and I pose no threat to you." It is also interesting to note that the chick is exhibiting no fear towards its gentle giant of a friend. Generally speaking, the very large breeds — Irish

Wolfhounds, Great Pyrenees, Greater Swiss Mountain Dogs and St. Bernards — seem to be aware of their great size, and compensate by being extremely gentle.

HUMAN PACK MEMBERS

Sociable by nature, dogs make the transition into our world with relative ease. Their natural pack instincts are easily transferred from the canine world to the human household. This is particularly true if a dog is introduced into a household as a young puppy. In this instance, the puppy views her owner as the pack leader, and the other family members as littermates. You can develop an even closer bond with your canine comrade by interacting with her on her level. By getting down on your hands and knees, you'll encourage her to play and relate to you as she would with others of her species.

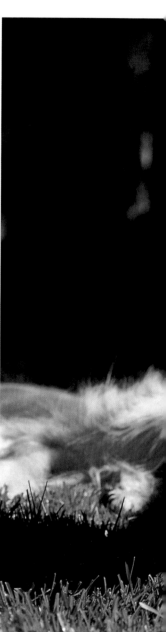

COMPANIONSHIP IN THE GOLDEN YEARS

While people of all ages derive wonderful rewards from dog ownership, senior citizens derive special benefits. Dogs provide loving, full-time companionship when friends and family are no longer around. The responsibility of dog ownership gives seniors a reason to get up and dressed in the morning — to feed and walk their canine companions. And for those older people who do not have the energy to run after and potty train a frisky little puppy, an older dog is the ideal solution. Generally less likely to be adopted than puppies and younger dogs, a more sedate, house-broken older dog will greatly appreciate living out her golden years in loving care.

THE SENIOR DOG

Many similarities exist between the aging process in humans and the aging process in dogs. For instance, a sign of aging common to both is the graying of the hair around the head. In dogs, this is particularly apparent around the muzzle and ears. Both older people and older dogs are likely to experience the stiffness associated with arthritis of the joints. And just as with older people, older dogs are prone to losing a portion or all of their eyesight and their hearing. Finally, without proper dental care, both species are prone to gum disease and tooth loss. That's why it's so important to brush your dog's teeth and have regular dental check ups throughout life. By doing so, your dog will be able to enjoy rawhide bones and chew toys — like this old lady here — right through her golden years.

DOGS
IN SERVICE
TO MAN

Many people owe their very lives to the work that dogs perform, particularly in the military, and in civilian rescue efforts. For other people, the services dogs provide vastly improve the quality of their lives, and enable them to participate actively in society.

THE DOG AS SOLDIER

As long as there have been wars, dogs have fought loyally at their masters' sides. During the early Middle Ages large and powerful war dogs were used to launch charges against the enemy. By more modern times, the development of the cavalry and the invention of firearms ended the need to use dogs for attack purposes.

Rather than emphasizing brute strength and aggressive tendencies, today's military dogs are selected for their intelligence and resourcefulness, patience and perseverance, mental and physical endurance, and dependability. Conditioned for battle, military dogs are taught to ignore gunfire, and are trained to run beneath bullets, shells, gas and flames during the execution of their duties.

Taught to distinguish the enemy by scent and sound, military dogs often serve as scouts on patrols preceding the troops. Trained to work in silence in order more easily to detect snipers and ambushes, these dogs have saved countless lives by alerting the troops to the enemy's presence. Other dogs serve as sentries, keeping watch over arms or munitions depots, aircraft hangers, and technical laboratories. Still others work as messengers, traveling silently at night, and bypassing any group of men except the one including their handlers. Due to their keen sense of smell, some military dogs are used in life-saving mine detection work, and the medical corps rely on casualty dogs to seek out the wounded and dead. Finally, specially trained parachute dogs, as their name suggests, actually jump from aircraft. Once safely on the ground, they join their handlers to resume their patrol and mine-detection work.

DOGS IN LAW ENFORCEMENT

Dogs are trained for a myriad of law enforcement purposes. Some specialize in detecting drugs, bombs, and contraband. Others are trained to search for criminals, and hold suspects at bay until arrests can be made. Some dogs serve as a second set of ears and as back-up for the lone police officer

FARM HAND

This Rough Collie has been bred for his agility and ingenuity in negotiating the narrow sheep paths of Scotland, and his luxurious coat protects him from the rigors of the climate of his native land. Under his straight outer coat lies a dense undercoat offering insulation from the blazing summer sun and the driving rains and snows of winter. Today, the Collie continues to herd sheep worldwide, and is also known for its accomplishments in military and police work.

During the fierce Arctic winter, teams of Siberian Huskies, Alaskan Malamutes and Samoyeds are harnessed to pull sleds across snow-covered territory, while in summer, when the snow is unfit for sleds, they are often used as pack animals. Favored for their strength and endurance, these three breeds feature dense undercoats that provide insulation from the harsh elements. Although the snowmobile has replaced the dog sled as a means of transportation in many areas, these dogs continue to be used in the sport of sled dog racing.

walking a beat, others are specially trained to work in crowds of people to maintain order and to control riots, while yet others are trained to track missing children, or to locate and rescue the victims of earthquakes, mud slides, and other disasters.

There are actually very few differences between law enforcement and military dogs. The same breeds are used, as well as the same discipline, and very nearly the same training procedures. Sadly, the main difference is the military dog's greater risk of being wounded or killed on duty.

PERFORMING TASKS FOR THE PHYSICALLY DISABLED

We are all familiar with guide dogs specially trained to serve as "eyes" for the blind. Taught to alert their owners to obstacles either by making a detour, or sitting down to warn them of the danger ahead, their training also includes learning how to judge the height of overhanging obstructions. Less well known, but just as vital, are hearing-ear dogs who are trained to respond to sources of sound for the hearing-impaired.

Remarkably, some dogs can be specially trained to respond to their owner's impending epileptic seizure. These dogs seem to possess an uncanny ability to sense the onset of an attack moments before it actually occurs – even before the owner is aware of it! Upon sensing the seizure's approach, a dog will direct his owner to a chair or other safe area and by doing so, greatly reduces the possibility of the owner sustaining injuries.

Other dogs have been taught to stand over their fallen owners and expose neck tags stating from which health problems the owner is suffering, and what emergency steps must be taken. For epileptics, and anyone requiring a safety pull cord to alert paramedics, dogs can be trained to pull these cords when their owners fall or cannot be aroused.

DOGS AS THERAPISTS

In addition to providing practical physical assistance to the disabled, dogs play an important role in a relatively new area of treatment called "pet facilitated therapy." Like other pets, dogs provide positive emotional benefits for the elderly, and the physically and emotionally disabled; they give love, offer companionship, and make their owners feel responsible and needed in maintaining their pets' care. Even people confined to hospitals and nursing homes benefit from visits from these "four-footed therapists." Much has been written about how patients' spirits are lifted, and how blood pressure is actually lowered, when people come in contact with pets. And dogs, whether they are trained to perform entertaining tricks or are simply stroked by the patients, make important contributions in this area.

PULLING HIS OWN WEIGHT

In many parts of the world, working dogs are still used in much the same way as horses — pulling carts, and as pack animals carrying people's burdens. These tasks require dogs that are strong, muscular, and sound. In some areas of Belgium, for example, draft dogs are harnessed by milkmen, butchers, fruit and vegetable vendors, bakers, and coal dealers. In Holland, draft dogs, such as the Newfoundland pictured here, still pull the carts of flower vendors. And years ago, travelling photographers earned a living by selling photographs of the local children posed in the carts.

BEAUTIFUL BACK PACKER

With its gorgeous white coat, the Samoyed is the most glamorous of all working dogs. Named after the Samoyed tribe of Siberia, it has lived and worked with people on the desolate Arctic steppes for centuries. This hardy breed has been a helper to reindeer herdsmen, and worked as a sled and pack dog. Working day after day under the coldest of winter conditions, they are known to draw one and a half times their own weight in supplies.

HORSE POWER

Arctic sled dogs have been bred for centuries as work dogs pulling heavy loads. It is important, therefore, to keep this hard-working heritage in mind should you choose one of these breeds as a pet. They need an incredible amount of exercise in order to expend their natural energy, otherwise behavioral problems may develop. It's also important to remember that their insulating coats are ideal for cooler climates but they'll need plenty of shade and water in warmer areas.

TO   THE   RESCUE

One of the regular exercises demanded of avalanche rescue dogs is to find a person buried in a deep hole. The St. Bernard, the most legendary of alpine rescue dogs, was bred by monks to assist in mountain rescue. Not given any special training, the young dogs were merely allowed to run with the older dogs on patrols during and following blizzards. If they came upon a storm victim, two dogs would lie down close by the victim to warm him, one of them licking his face to restore consciousness. Another dog, in the meantime, would return to the monastery to alert the monks and guide them to the scene. Today, St. Bernards have been joined by German Shepherds and other breeds for this life-saving work.

LOCATING   THE   MISSING

Avalanches are not the only occasions when dogs prove themselves invaluable in service to mankind. Because of their highly developed sense of smell, dogs can detect odors so faint that they are imperceptible to us and they can identify and locate a person by simply being exposed to some object the individual has worn or handled. Many people lost in forests or rugged terrain owe their lives to the efforts of these search-and-rescue dogs. In landslides and other disasters in which it is necessary to detect and free people buried under debris, rescue dogs enable us to save a great deal of time and effort. Once trained, these dogs indicate the results of their search or their discoveries by showing very different reactions if the victims are alive or dead.

◄ *Police departments and law enforcement agencies all over the world rely on dogs to assist them in their efforts. It takes a special kind of dog to work in law enforcement. Because they are in constant contact with the public, they have to be hard and firm with criminals, yet perfectly natural and friendly with others; they must possess the ability to become hostile upon command, and just as quickly revert to their basic good natures once their tasks have been completed. Dogs involved in law enforcement go through an extensive period of specialized training. If they are to be used in criminal work, they are trained to chase and detain, defend their human partners or themselves if necessary, and even disarm criminals bearing weapons. Their training also teaches them to become accustomed to gunfire, and to intimidating situations such as threatened beatings. Finally, because their senses of hearing and smell are so acute, law enforcement agencies rely on these dogs for searching unfamiliar buildings and areas in order to locate criminals, or missing persons.*

◀ With his keen intelligence and highly developed senses, the German Shepherd is considered by many to be the most utilitarian dog of all. He serves in many roles in our society — defender, drug-detector, guard, life-saver, sentry, tracker, guide for the blind — just to name a few. Probably the most famous German Shepherd ever was Rin Tin Tin, Hollywood's canine movie star who delighted audiences throughout the world with his heroic acts. The little fellow pictured here won't be a film star but he may well be a hero some day. Once he's completed months of extensive police training, he'll be assigned to walk a beat with a two-footed patrolman. Who knows how many missing children he'll locate, criminals he'll help capture, and lives he'll help save!

EMPLOYING THAT SENSITIVE NOSE

◀ When it comes to the detection of drugs and other contraband, nothing surpasses the accuracy of a well-trained dog. Used to sniff out illegal shipments, dogs are responsible for the seizure of tons of marijuana and cocaine, and the arrests of thousands of smugglers every year worldwide. No human or machine can do this job as quickly or as efficiently as these dogs with their highly developed olfactory senses. Interestingly enough, dogs also put their noses at the service of gourmets in a similar fashion — specially trained truffle dogs are used to unearth this expensive culinary delicacy. Unlike pigs which are sometimes also used to render this service, truffle dogs offer an advantage — they don't eat the truffles once they find them!

A FORBIDDING PRESENCE

Quick, intelligent, agile, and strong — the Doberman Pincher is a born guard dog. Like other dogs, his abilities as a sentinel stem from his natural instinct to defend his territory and to protect his owner. Guard dogs are ideal for private and industrial security, particularly in smaller operations which cannot afford elaborate security systems. They have been used successfully to patrol department stores after hours to control the losses inflicted by "sleep-ins" (burglars who enter the store shortly before closing time, remain overnight stealing merchandise, then depart the next morning soon after the store opens).

Just like personal pets and their owners, military working dogs can develop strong bonds with their handlers, upon whom they rely for feeding, grooming, exercise and play.

The military working dog's initial obedience training does not differ significantly from that of personal pets: both require patience and firmness, and are based on repetition, reward, and correction. Once his basic obedience training has been

completed, the military dog's special advanced training begins. During this, he is taught to ride quietly in patrol vehicles without demonstrating hostility to other people or dogs, and to search for suspects in buildings and open areas. As part of his training the military dog learns how to attack without command anyone who is threatening his handler, and quickly to cease such an attack upon being commanded to do so.

Perhaps the most noble and important service dogs provide for mankind is their aid to the disabled. Although most of us are familiar with seeing-eye dogs who are trained to guide the blind, it is important to remember that this is not the only task dogs are trained to perform for the disabled. They can be trained to serve as "ears" for those who cannot hear, for instance, or as an extra pair of "hands" and/or "legs" for those confined to wheelchairs. In fact, every day, thousands of people with all types of disabilities rely on their specially trained dogs in order to maintain their independence, and to function fully in society. Performing everyday tasks that many people take for granted — opening doors, retrieving dropped items, alerting owners when the doorbell rings — these dogs can mean the difference between a person living independently on his own or having to exist in an institutional setting.

THE GOOD SHEPHERDS

Herding sheep is no easy chore. Canine shepherds must move the flock along the road, make it string out when a car approaches, run alongside to keep members from straying, and follow it in order to keep it moving. Once at the pasture, the dogs must watch over their charges, keeping them within the limits of their territory, rounding up the strays — and all the while watching for predators. Some breeds have developed their own herding styles. Take the short-legged Welsh Corgi pictured here. He herds by biting the heels of his charges, then drops to the ground to avoid being kicked. Other dogs will actually jump on flock members' backs to cut off or turn back a runaway. In fact, some of these dogs are so skillful that they compete in formal trials throughout the world.

INDEX

Photographic acknowledgments
Animal Photography/Sally-Anne Thompson p8, 9, 78; Norvia Behling p16 (bottom), 36, 45, 48, 49, 50, 53, 56, 62, 63 (bottom), 72, 113, 122, 126; Mike Blair, K.S. Hutchinson, Dr Johnson p86, 87; Pam Brackett p55 (top); Kent & Donna Dannen p14, 35, 69, 71, 75, 81, 89, 91, 100, 111, 116, 117 (top) 119; Department of Defense/United States of America p123; Jane Faircloth p18, 27, 30, 32, 74, 109; F.P.G. International/Larry Grant p21; F.P.G. International/M. Rothwill p20 (bottom); F.P.G. International/J. Taposchaner p51, 65; F.P.G. International/John Terence Turner p64; F.P.G. International/C.J. Zimmerman p38; Russ Gutschall p120 (top); Marc Henrie p2, 3, 11, 28, 44, 66, 80, 90, 112, 120 (bottom); Willie L. Hill p125; Itti Bitti Design p59, 76; Nick Jones p58; Gary Kramer p88; Ron Kimball p15 (bottom), 11, 16, (top), 20 (top), 25, 29, 30, 34, 41 47, 55 (bottom), 95, 97, 98, 101, 102, 103, 106 (top), 107, 114; Lon E Lauber p42; Ronald Levy p17, 33, 39, 54, 61, 104 (top), 105, 108, 124; Joe McDonald p84, 92, 93 (top); M.A. McDonald p85, 93 (bottom); Frank Mantlik p15 (top), 43; Steve Maslowski p18; Metropolitan Police p121; Profiles West p127; Profiles West/Tim Haske p23, 104 (bottom), 106 (bottom); Profiles West/P. Barry Levy p110; Profiles West/Burnett/Winsett p118; Profiles West/Peggy Daly p68; Profiles West/Allen Russell p26, 60; Profiles West/Bob Winsett p57; Mae Scanlan p90; Dale Spartas p1, 7, 13, 22, 24, 40, 67, 77, 99; Telephoto/William D. Adams p63 (top); Telephoto/Chris Minerva p52; John W. Warden p70, 115, 117 (bottom); Wheeler Pictures/John Dominus p37; 79; Michael Work p83 (bottom), 83 (top).